# Crocodile or Alligator
## Which Is Which?

By Tamra B. Orr



21st Century **Junior** Library

Published in the United States of America by
**Cherry Lake Publishing**
Ann Arbor, Michigan
www.cherrylakepublishing.com

Reading Adviser: Marla Conn, MS, Ed., Literacy specialist, Read-Ability, Inc.
Content Adviser: Susan Heinrichs Gray

Photo Credits: ©Vladimir Wrangel/Shutterstock, cover (left); ©DavidAdamsTX/Shutterstock, cover (right); ©Arto Hakola/Shutterstock, 4; ©Craig Russell/Shutterstock, 6; ©Rudy Umans/Shutterstock, 8; ©Mauricio Acosta Rojas/Shutterstock, 10; ©Marc Pletcher/Shutterstock, 12; ©Svetlana Foote/Shutterstock, 14; ©EcoPrint/Shutterstock, 16, 18; ©Nicole S Glass/Shutterstock, 20



Library of Congress Cataloging-in-Publication Data

Names: Orr, Tamra, author.
Title: Crocodile or alligator / Tamra B. Orr.
Description: Ann Arbor : Cherry Lake Publishing, [2019] | Series: Which is which? | Includes bibliographical references and index. | Audience: K to Grade 3.
Identifiers: LCCN 2019005991 | ISBN 9781534147317 (hardcover) | ISBN 9781534150171 (paperback) | ISBN 9781534148741 (pdf) | ISBN 9781534151604 (hosted ebook)
Subjects: LCSH: Crocodiles—Juvenile literature. | Alligators—Juvenile literature.
Classification: LCC QL666.C925 O77 2019 | DDC 597.98/2—dc23
LC record available at https://lccn.loc.gov/2019005991

Cherry Lake Publishing would like to acknowledge the work of the Partnership for 21st Century Skills. Please visit *www.p21.org* for more information.

Printed in the United States of America
Corporate Graphics

# CONTENTS

Alligators are smaller than crocodiles.

# A Matter of Snout

“See you later, alligator!”

“In a while, crocodile!”

Do these sayings make you think crocodiles and alligators are the same animal? They aren’t! In fact, people often confuse one for the other. Both are large **reptiles** with tough, scaly skin. They are **cold-blooded**. They bury their eggs in sand or in a pile of plant matter. They swim in water by sweeping their long tails from side to side. Both animals also have big, sharp teeth.

Crocodiles weigh twice as much as alligators!

Look closer. Can you spot the differences? Can you tell which is which?

Start with their **snouts**. An alligator's snout is wide and U-shaped. A crocodile's snout is narrow and V-shaped. If a crocodile's mouth is closed, you can see an upward-pointing tooth near the front of its snout.

Alligators also usually only grow up to 15 feet (5 meters) long. They weigh 1,000 pounds (453 kilograms) or less than crocodiles. Crocodiles can grow up to 23 feet (7 m) long.

## Make a Guess!

Both alligators and crocodiles swim with their eyes and noses on top of the water. This way, they can see where they are going. Why else would they not swim under the water?

American alligators can live for 30 to 50 years.

# Fresh or Salty?

Here's another clue for telling the difference between an alligator and crocodile. Check its **habitat**. There are about 3 million alligators in the United States. American alligators are found in the southern states, such as Louisiana, Florida, and Texas. They like the freshwater found in ponds, streams, lakes, and rivers. The only other **species** of alligator lives along China's Yangtze River valley. This alligator is far smaller than the American alligator.

Larger crocodiles are known to live for as long as 60 to 70 years!

There are fewer than 2,000 crocodiles in the United States. Unlike alligators, crocodiles are found all over the world. They live everywhere, from Africa, Australia, and Asia to South America and Central America. Crocodiles are different from alligators in another way. They are perfectly happy living in lakes, rivers, and saltwater! Their tongues can **filter** out the salt so it does not bother them.

## Ask Questions!

The only place in the United States where alligators and crocodiles live side by side is Florida. What makes Florida a good place for them to live? Look up the state online and see what clues you can find.

Female alligators can lay over 50 eggs in a season. They also tend to stay with their young for as long as 3 years.

# Mammals Beware!

Alligators and crocodiles are different. But they want the same things when they get hungry. After hatching from their eggs, these young reptiles eat worms and insects. As adults, both animals want something bigger. Their sharp teeth come in handy. They will snack on frogs, fish, turtles, and birds. Their jaws are extremely strong. They can even bring down a deer or buffalo!

Female crocodiles and alligators carry their young
to the water in their mouths!

Alligators and crocodiles don't chew their food. Instead, they tear off chunks of meat and swallow them in one gulp. If a tooth falls out or breaks, these reptiles just grow another one.

Will alligators or crocodiles attack people? The answer is yes. But this doesn't usually happen. Like other **predators**, these reptiles only attack people if they feel they are being threatened.

## Look!

*Deinosuchus* means "terrible crocodile." **Fossils** from this crocodile have been found from Mexico to Montana. This creature lived up to 80 million years ago. Its skull was more than 6.5 feet (2 m) long. Its body was between 30 and 40 feet (9 and 12 m) long. Imagine if reptiles were still that large!

Alligators and crocodiles can actually shed tears. However, these tears are there to clean and moisten their eyes and not soothe their sadness.

# Fast and Strong

Alligators and crocodiles have been on earth for more than 200 million years! This might be because they're skillful hunters. Their eyes have **vertical** pupils that open wide in low light. This gives them great night vision. They also have a sharp sense of hearing and smell. They can even hold their breath up to an hour! This helps them hide

Crocodiles can survive several months without food.

underwater. All of these abilities make it easy to sneak up on **prey**.

These reptiles are also quite fast in water. This is because they both have strong tails. By moving their tail back and forth, crocodiles can swim up to 9 miles (14 kilometers) per hour. Alligators can go as fast as 20 miles (32 km) per hour! On land, both reptiles are slower. This is because of their short legs and heavy bodies. However, they are still able to **sprint** about 10 to 15 miles (16 to 24 km) per hour.

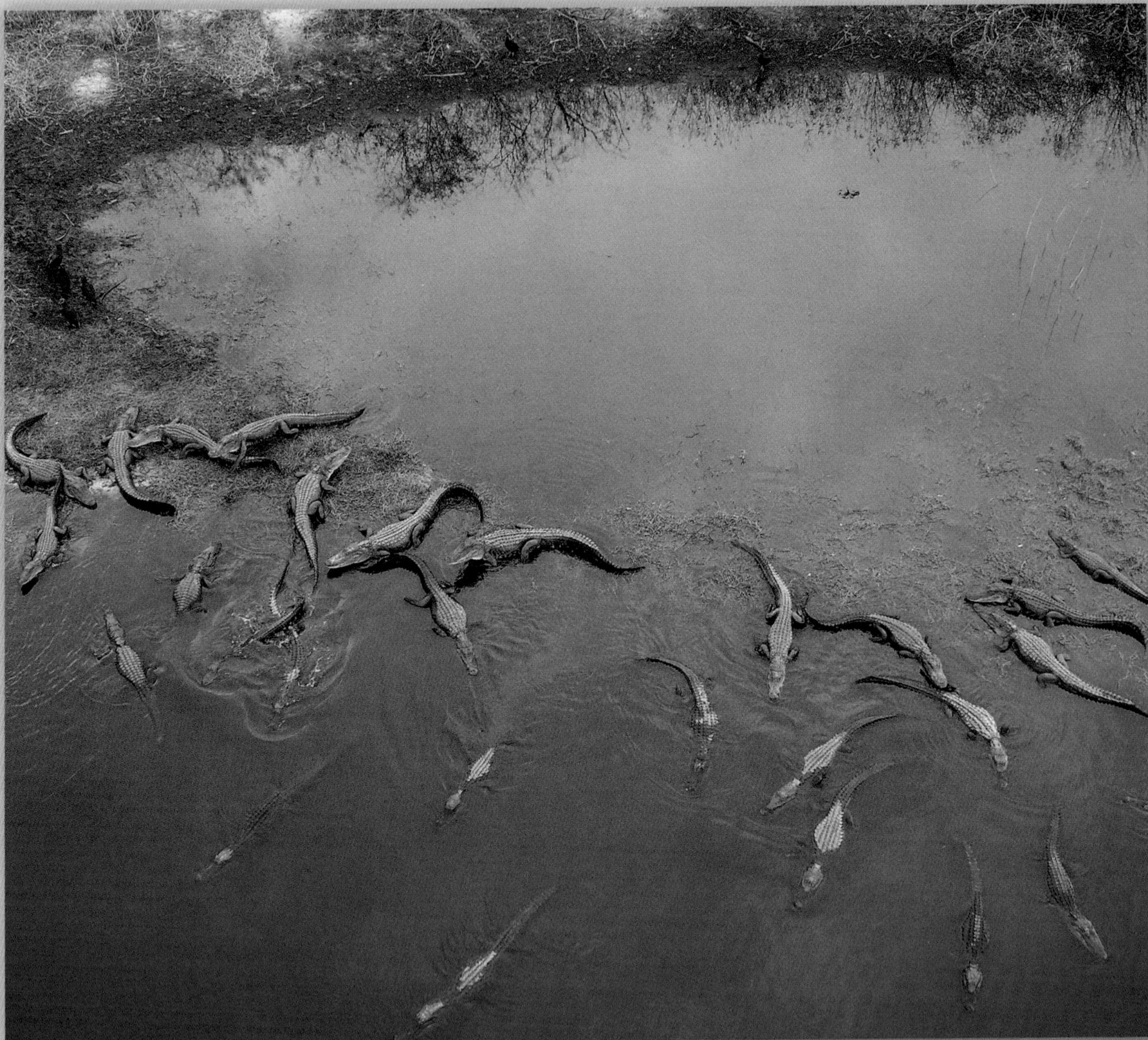

During extremely hot or cold weather, alligators will stay in a "gator hole" and slow down their body. This is called brumation.

Crocodiles and alligators are not the same, but they are both fascinating. They are some of the oldest and most interesting species in the world!

## Think!

Alligators and crocodiles have another hunting trick. The alligator has black spots on its jaw. The crocodile has them all over its body. These spots help the reptile feel tiny changes in the water. Why do you think a crocodile might notice more changes than an alligator?

# GLOSSARY

**cold-blooded** (kohld-BLUHD-id) having a body temperature that cannot be controlled and that changes with the animal's surroundings

**filter** (FIL-tur) to remove unwanted material

**fossils** (FAH-suhlz) the remains of an ancient animal or plant preserved in rock

**habitat** (HAB-ih-tat) area where an animal lives

**predators** (PRED-uh-turz) animals that live by hunting other animals for food

**prey** (PRAY) an animal that is hunted or killed by another animal for food

**reptiles** (REP-tilez) animals with dry, scaly skin and soft-shelled eggs, such as lizards, snakes, crocodiles, and alligators

**snouts** (SNOUTS) the long front part of an animal's head that includes its nose, mouth, and jaws

**species** (SPEE-sheez) a group of animals that are similar and can produce young animals

**sprint** (SPRINT) to run a short distance quickly

**vertical** (VUR-tih-kuhl) up and down, rather than left to right

# FIND OUT MORE

## BOOKS

Jackson, Tom. *World's Deadliest Reptiles*. Minneapolis, MN: Hungry Tomato, 2019.

Marcos, Victoria. *Discover Alligators and Crocodiles.* Irvine, CA: Xist Publishing, 2018.

Mattern, Joanne. *Alligators and Crocodiles.* Egremont, MA: Red Chair Press, 2017.

Read, Tracy. *Exploring the World of Alligators and Crocodiles.* Buffalo, NY: Firefly Books, 2017.

Williams, Jake. *Remarkable Reptiles.* New York, NY: Sterling Children's Books, 2018.

## WEBSITES

**Ducksters—Alligators and Crocodiles**
https://www.ducksters.com/animals/alligatorcrocodile.php
Learn more about the differences between alligators and crocodiles.

**Easy Science for Kids—Alligator vs Crocodile Facts for Kids Video**
https://easyscienceforkids.com/alligator-vs-crocodile-facts-for-kids-video
Watch and learn more fun facts about alligators and crocodiles.

# INDEX



## ABOUT THE AUTHOR

Tamra Orr is the author of hundreds of books for readers of all ages. She graduated from Ball State University, but moved with her husband and four children to Oregon in 2001. She is a full-time author, and when she isn't researching and writing, she writes letters to friends all over the world. Orr enjoys life in the big city of Portland and feels very lucky to read about dangerous reptiles but not be too close to any of them.